Singing from Silence

Singing from Silence

poetry by
Jane Downes

Polished Stone Publishing
P.O. Box 2202
Sebastopol, CA 95473

Cover image: Taylor Hawke
Art direction: Katherine A. Dieter
Cover & interior layout: Lesley Thornton-Raymond

Previously published:

"*In Luxembourg Gardens,*" George Square Poetry, Edinburgh University, 1969

"*Hiking In,*" Quarry, UC Santa Barbara, 1972

"*Eternal Now, A Great Love, The Secret, Equinox, and Dare We Imagine*" appear in the book *Waking Up* by Taylor Hawke, The Printed Voice, 2014

ISBN: 978-0-9980976-3-3
Printed in the USA on acid free paper
10 9 8 7 6 5 4 3 2

Table of Contents

Foreword

This book of Jane Downes' poetry—*Singing from Silence*—is being published posthumously (1947-2017).

Jane had been preparing to publish this book for several years. It was nearly complete when she was diagnosed with pancreatic cancer, and her attention went to other pressing concerns.

Jane and I met eighteen years ago, and have been close ever since—partners for several years, then dear friends, and long-time collaborators. I was one of Jane's caregivers in her final weeks. During that time, she shared her wish that her poetry be published, and asked me to help.

It has been my privilege to shepherd Jane's book of poetry through the publishing process. It started 18 years ago, when she showed me a small box. Inside were many pieces of paper—all handwritten poems that she had been writing and collecting.

I entered them all in the computer, helped her organize and edit them, and provided other support along the way. And Jane had been editing, reorganizing, and polishing this book of poems ever since then. Now, as she wished, the rest of the publishing process is complete.

Taylor Hawke, Author
Waking Up: Consciousness, Culture and Climate Solutions (2015 Atlas Award Winner)
Edited by Jane Downes

Acknowledgments

I honor and thank Werner Erhard for his masterful teaching and mentoring, for my initial transformational experience, and for the privilege of serving and being contributed to by so many through that work.

My heart of appreciation to Swami Muktananda, Gurumayi, Swami Durgananda, all of whom gave the grace of shakti and beautiful guidance.

To Deepak Chopra, for his Seduction of Spirit program which re-introduced me after many years to meditation and the inner world.

To Ramana Maharshi, and to Gangaji who introduced me to Ramana. The depth of inquiry and joy of your presence and teachings live on.

To Master Tung, my Tai Chi sifu, for your unceasing quiet teaching, allowing for the possibility of embodiment.

To the Dali Lama, Thich Nhat Hahn, and Mother Meera whose presence at this time fosters and demonstrates light and peace regardless of world events.

To my poet teachers Hafiz, Rilke, Rumi, St. John of the Cross, Wendell Berry, ee.cummings, Blake, Yeats, and David Whyte, all of whom shine the light beyond language in their work, and continue to inspire all.

To compassionate and generous support by Daniel Ladinsky, a wonderful teacher and translator of Hafiz and other mystics.

To my parents Nancy and Bob Palmer for their love and fostering of my creativity, to all of my teachers whose support made possible these expressions, and to Taylor Hawke whose encouragement and plain hard work formatting, editing and listening allowed this work to come to fruition.

Introduction

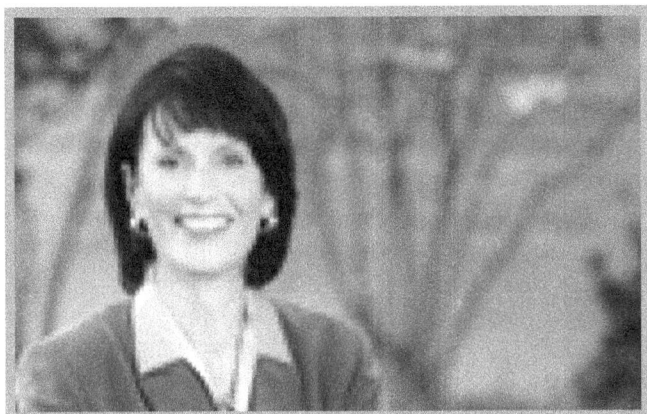

No one can understand the true value of silence unless they have a real respect for the validity of language: for the reality which is expressible in language is found, face to face and without medium, in silence. Nor would we find this reality in itself, that is to say in its own silence, unless we were first brought there by language.

—Thomas Merton

Dear Reader,

It is my wish that these poems encourage and support all of us in making friends with silence, and thus with our souls and with God. May all our speech and action be informed by this deeper communion.

We live at a time when the pull to distraction by externals is unprecedented, and grows daily. We are constantly bombarded by not only our internal chatter, but a cacophony of phone calls, leaf blowers, cars, planes, television and so on. Some expressions of art can provide a still place of sanctuary in a world where silence and stillness of any kind have become rare and undervalued. It is my intent that this small work be such a place of peace.

The poetry here is a product of engaging in the improbable challenge of attempting to speak from the ever-deepening silence that came calling.

Some years ago, during a time of intensely active teaching, travel and commitment, I met a wonderful shaman in Mexico. She said I must write poems about the experience of meditation. I was puzzled by the statement, and dismissed the thought.

A few years after leaving public life, the poems began to come. I grew to love and find joy in this absurd calling of putting into words that which is ultimately beyond all language. Doomed to failure at the start, a playful approach appeared, and the work came to be about the possibility of finding threads of light that might be woven in between the lines. Finding those threads in daily living became the real journey and the writing itself a kind of meditation.

I recall just at the beginning of this work, a sweet moment of slowing down into stillness at the edge of the McKenzie River in Oregon where my father was fishing.

I simply stood at the edge of the riverbank and was carried away, weeping in joy, simply being in the still presence of Nature. From then on, each poem came as a kind of revelation and teaching, a gift. Some of them I am still learning to live into.

Though we don't often speak of it, there is something within each of us that seeks nourishment through love of the sublime. This impetus expresses itself in many different ways. For some it happens as a moment in the beauty of nature, for others in holding a young infant, or hearing an inspiring song, and of course in mystical and spiritual experiences as expressed by saints and sages through time. We all have access to this experience even in midst of our ordinary living, and with work we can listen, refine and deepen it.

Perhaps, through sharing these poems, in a moment of communion, we may come to touch that ultimate dimension which can resonate throughout our lives. To live through the eyes and heart of what gives a poem life, in that place where "seeing sees itself," this is poetry as a kind of yoga, or union.

> *Your innermost sense of self, of who you are, is inseparable from stillness. This is the "I am" that is deeper than name and form…when you become aware of silence, immediately there is that state of inner still alertness. You are present. You have stepped out of thousands of years of collective human conditioning.*
>
> *—Eckhart Tolle*

Life today tends to be complex and the tensions in the world situation loom large. Ultimately this disharmony is based in our sense of separation. Our apparent differences in culture, religion, gender, race, and class can seem insurmountable barriers to peace, harmony and community. Given our times, I have been moved to serve up, in some small way, a taste of our true sameness, of our oneness.

May these words serve as a kind of invocation, and your reading of them nourish your aware connection with that stillness which gives life to all.

The poetry here is in celebration and wonder of an ever-present, always available grace in which we all dwell. I offer it to you with gratitude to my teachers, and to all teachers, who have taught, and continue to do so, in silence. And of course, to the Nameless One—teacher of all teachers.

Peace,
Jane

If the outer world is diminished in its grandeur then the emotional, imaginative, intellectual, and spiritual life of the human is diminished or extinguished. Without the soaring birds, the great forests, the sounds and coloration of the insects, the free-flowing streams, the flowering fields, the sight of the clouds by day and the stars at night, we become impoverished in all that makes us human.

–*Thomas Berry, The Great Work*

·

THE SECRET

We live within
this great Mystery
and it within us;
the way salmon
swim the secret waters
which flow invisibly into
and through them.

Awakening
as this secret,
we too surrender,
and are carried
not only down, but upstream
leaping high,
up and out of rapids,
lifting beyond logic,
toward our true
spawning grounds.

In this passage,
we discover, if only
for a short passionate time,
the shock, not only of air
but of water,
and whatever gives
this instinct to swim
toward Source,
this being drawn
inexorably to where

(in a kind of ultimate
thrashing),

we finally
give it all up.

Here,
having relinquished
everything,
emerges
that radiant peace
which lies
(a silent secret)
within
and without.

RAIN SONG

Today it's in the gentle essence
of rain, this constant quiet drizzle
harmonizing with the notes
of larger drops, dripping
from the tile roof
tap-tapping as they land,
teaching the joy of the fall.

It's in the essence
between those drops,
the Silence,
that makes a song at all;
and in the soft radiance,
subtly intensifying
as sunlight breaks through, briefly
illuminating this fluid dance.

It lies in the dark deep place
between new blades
of emerald green grass
emerging at last in the fertile
richness of thls damp effulgence,
this long awaited cleansing.

A single frog celebrates it now,
singing in warm wetness.
Between each croak,
between each water-note
a kind of quiet descends:
the kind of quiet that falls
only when one has been awake
and waiting (a very) long time,

and at last, in a downpour
it all comes home.

Listen, these are yours,
these rain-seeds of silence,
opening to a deeper peace
which dances within,
the way notes
of a truly sacred song
reverberate
long after the music
is gone.

PRAISE

Perhaps all poetry is simply praise,
the eye raising skyward today,
later pulls the hawk onto this page,
sings in awe of feathers fanning
wide against bright sky and prays
for its circle of flight to emerge again,
here, evoked now anew in you.

How we long to praise it all:
each moment a poem.

Or to simply say that today
beneath light blue fields of sky,
and such elegant flight,
Spring in her finest profusion
is wild with green, unspeakable
shades layered between
shocks of yellow mustard.

Once it begins it has no end,
this full praise. Praise today!
This, a delicate reunion
over tea and poetry—
every room, every move
a reminder of exquisite touch,
so much,
only a breath away,
yet later nothing is said of this,
walking in silence at dusk,
brushing knee deep
through greens and yellows.

Such intimacy, while knowing
now a deeper bliss,
the still One, deeper than any kiss:
the One
that survives the inevitable loss of all
human loves, the One that lives beyond
all bonds of belonging, of "I" and "Mine",
the One that goes on now
echoing in silence,
beyond all time.

Praise it All!

the Infinite, even now in time.
hanging here in a small diamond-drop
of dew, as it sparkles
on the silver thread a spider wove—

drawing an illusory line, so that each
might feel comfortable seeming
to be left behind, as the car pulls away,
breaking the web, loosing the dew.

So too shall the praising go on, knowing
now that nothing is ever really unsaid,
and that the threads of joy and sorrow
lead always to a quiet place, where
beyond words, they meet in peace.

Standing here
at last
in silence

Praise it All!

THE LIGHT IN ALL THINGS

The light in all things
shines through seemingly
separate threads of all that is:

misery and bliss
solid granite and even
this tiny blade of grass;
the sweet breath of the infant
and the aged one's gentle kiss,

all seems woven into one brilliant tapestry

even the trash-bin,
yesterday's smudged news
scuddering loose in the wind,
and the dark asphalt beneath,

all shine with this light.

From the constant buzz of traffic, to
cries of war and stillness of peace;
deep shades of caterpillar fuzz
and tender-veined butterfly wings

all are rendered whole in this light.

The toothless man
sleeping on cardboard
in a darkened stoop,
rests radiant behind it all;

waxy narcissus and cactus,
gleam within, and far beyond,
a wide ocean at mid-day shimmers
in trillions of tiny ripples:
a motion of liquid light.

Sometimes late at night
along the coast, phosphorescent
blue-tinged waves burst up
out of the dark shore
dissolving, falling back again
into black sea.

All ordinary moments shine too:

In the kitchen
just chopping broccoli—
shimmering green droplets
slip lightly off the knife
as the gleaming blade
pierces tough stems.

And over there,
that "other" person
seeming so separate
and apart,
just there beyond
any variation in shade
of our frail skin;
beyond any difference
in gender or opinion,
faith, politics or culture
we all shine alike within:
being One
in both blood and light.

Even in the darkest hour of night
when all hope seems drained away;
when despair and fear threaten
to bind it all--just there--lies
a light, a peace, which un-minding,
heals,
        illuminating all,

        a light beyond darkness,
                a light beyond the light.
        Seer and seen,
        one source,

        emanating
        as the light
        in all things.

NATARAJA: SHIVA DANCING

In the garden,
beneath the thick, sweet
scent of nightshade lilies
Shiva dances an eternal dance:
the cosmos in dynamic motion,
captured in bronze.

Such statuesque movement,
at center of the flaming metal circle
outlasts all magnificent flowerings
and fragrances dangling above.

Shiva, symbol of this dance
of life and death, just by lifting
one foot, all are released from rebirth.
With a flaming halo circling your head,
you stand centered, calm,
unruffled by any display of energy,
even radical earthly changes.

The dwarf of ignorance,
lies crushed under foot,
leaving all forgetfulness
forever trampled out.
And above your matted hair
a crescent moon shines
with love, fertility, illumination.
while below, perfectly balanced
on one foot, you embody
the immortal way,
the path of liberation.

~   ~   ~   ~

Suddenly,
in shimmering moonlight,
Shiva seems to step out of his
bronze circle, spinning
across the garden.

Plants and insects and birds
arise for a moment and
join in, for it is night,
and no one is watching this
miraculous dance of bliss--
creating, sustaining, ultimately
destroying, only to create again.

For Shiva dances still
(now and will always)
within each of us.

Shiva,
dance on,
through time and form
shine your light.
Through lilies and roses
through war and lust,
love and compassion,
hatred and greed,
high and low;
through all things beautiful
and impermanent,
shine on
so that all may glow.

Dance this, your eternal dance,
beyond birth,
beyond death,
dance on Shiva,
dance on!

MATILIJA SANCTUARY: RIVER SPEAKS

Come sit close to me the river says,
Listen:
        every place has its pull,
        feel the pull of this place,
        the ancient tug
        toward peace.
        Let go, the way
        a boulder drops to bottom,
        soundlessly, slowly
        sinking down
        to river bed.
Listen:
        Let go, and find
        the silent center,
        feel from within
        the great weight,
        let it draw you
        toward that place
        where granite hits sand,
        and at last, stands still.
Listen:
        It says, come to rest here
        beneath the rush of it all,
        let currents wash
        above and around you,
        slip into the cool center,
        and immerse yourself
        in the hush, in the quiet
        knowledge of silence.

Come to the depths.
Come to rest
in this place where
rainbow fish hover,
flitting silver fins,
facing upstream
into the source,
as if suspended,
at rest, in this dark,
wet, shadow world
of stillness.

She says,
listen hard,
listen deep,
you must go
under
for this rare
river peace.

Plumb the depths,
sink into a peace
river rocks know,
yet can never say.

Only then
can you rise,
only then can you
surface,
breaking through,
up into the light,
breaking out,
into a sudden
rush of air,
and once there,

carry forever
the immutable secret,
silent and solid,
within
your open
heart.

SONG

This winter
snow settles
in palm fronds
and suddenly,
for the first time
I hear their songs:

> *birds hidden, singing*
> *as though the leaves*
> *themselves sang*

or as if somehow
I were one
with the source
of all singing and
the palm, my body,
     a brown naked trunk
     ringed with years
     plunging up
     into the green
from which I sing

invisible

THE CONTRACTOR

A tractor
        scars
the morning
        cutting
even into this poem;
grinding on for hours
        moving
as this pen moves:

        leveling here
pushing mounds up there
shearing the hill
for a road,
some building,

making space
a commodity.

                At night
                I
                am the phantom
                        healer
                mounting
                the cracked black seat
                of my silent tractor,
                shoving the gears,
                then rolling,
                I push
                        as I please,
                a sculptress in motion,
                filling
                        the day's holes,

leveling its hills
restoring each fallen
tree,
in noiseless
revolution
          putting Nature
back
          together.

EQUINOX

The first day of spring
and pollywogs now become
frogs leap from the pond below.
Fecund, this first day of spring
as it opens in glow of yellow daisies.
And above, each plum blossom's
fuzz shows soft baby-pink petals
around bright centers
now buzzing full with bees—
slow and heavy, laden
with their pollen gifts.

So much richness in all of this,
as we rest on soft green tufts of grass
beneath willow trees,
feeling the strong dark muscles
of roots and earth beneath.

Such abundance comes
as if by some invisible
sacred bond agreed upon
for this instant only—
life's longing for itself
fulfilled, yet never quite
done with its own longing—
each breath laden
with jasmine perfume
and cheeks cooled
by the invisible kiss
of a tender breeze.

Thus we open just as spring does,
in all its wild, yet ordered intensity,
opening wide and staying open
to this inexplicable attraction of love
for Love; feeling now in blood,
that ocean of energy in which we swim,
that same force which gently unfolds
each blossom.

In coming so alive
we sense deep in our bones,
in the soul of each moment,
the yearning of the universe
for an unleashing
of the beauty we now are;
and through this,
the entire cosmos
constantly expanding itself.

In such a time of reawakening,
we come to know again
our unique union with all of life,
the way the heron born in the high tree
on a California coast carries
the ocean air in her breast,
and the wind of that particular day
in her wings wherever she goes.

In this way, we too carry
soaring in our hearts
the longing of life
for its own unfolding;

and in a single moment of surrender
into the silent depths,
a luminous sense of fullness—
a union with the elegance
and mystery of our origins
awakens
as the universe
in this very moment's
pull toward being alive
as all of this:
Here.
Now.

(for Brian Swimme)

THE GARDEN

Planting
for the first time this spring
I found the damp sun-warm
earth under my hands
as comfortable as love's touch.
But the seeds in my palm seemed
such dry and dead things—
I pushed them down, burying
them in wet, darkness, and warmth.

Yet when I had finished,
blanketed seeds and stood,
something of that contact lingered
in more than a muddied hand.
And like a child, who
out of some hunger
repeats the newly learned,
I bent as if compelled,
and planted again and again;
not only marigolds but melons,
squash and corn, beans,
cucumber and onion, until all
the yard was turned to bed:
rows and mounds, stakes and string.

*　　*　　*　　*　　*

Now I come daily to the garden
as if more than mere seed
were buried here.
I kneel and scrutinize
each row, searching out

new shoots, the minutest
growth, and waiting.

I have never known a harvest,
never tried the earth.
And I wonder
about those tiny seeds, lying
like poems underground
while I wait.

RIDING

Now I can tell you
how as a girl
there were always summer horses
loping in and out
my fenceless dreams;
and how
I used to move with their thunder
willfully caught in the motion.
How over trimmed hedges, streams and logs
we leapt (brown mane mingled with brown
hair) and wind whipping red
into my cheeks.

How the flinching at flies,
pricked ears and
low whinny of pleasure
(even those bared teeth
and flattened ears)
were worth a single moment:

when the only pounding was not of hooves,
(breath heaving moist clouds
from pink nostrils,
dilated)
when heated we'd pause
in dry oak shade
to rest in the interim
of stillness
(white foam upon the neck)
trembling, as upon the crest
of motion,
breaking.

SNAIL LOVE

So rare, so sadly rare:
at last we are at rest
and slowed down.
Sunday in the garden,
slow enough even for
a surprise encounter,
slow enough
to see two snails
on the brick pavement
their soft mouths moving,
meshing together.

Strangely not unlike
human kissing, this
sensual, slippery
mating—one's neck
falling sideways,
surrendered beneath
the other's caress.

Watching entranced,
pulled into another
world, and taking time
to dive into the leisure,
into the oft-missed
touch of the moment,
we look up.

Without speaking
we understand
the snails' gift:
the courage to stop often,

to go slowly enough
in our daily living
and in our loving
not to miss

anything.

FULL MOON AND APPLES

September solstice
and the tree is laden,
full with yellow-gold apples,
hanging in tight clusters;
Golden Delicious heavy
on each bough, now bent
almost to breaking.

As we pick, reaching up,
gently tugging the ripe ones,
my father and I share
(mostly in silence) this
harvest he planted
years ago. Precious
now, our rare time
together, just this,
picking apples.

Mostly our love has been thus:
unspoken, a simple quiet
understanding, like the strong
tiny stem this huge fruit
somehow hangs from,
giving sustenance invisibly.

Tonight, before bed,
passing by the tree,
an apple-yellow moon
makes shadows, its
soft light falling
on the few small ones
we left to ripen.

In this moment,
I too am connected,
fresh and whole,
left hanging to grow again
into some unknown future,
yet certain that through
an invisible stem
we are somehow always fed
from the tree,
from the seed,
through which Life's
sweet-fullness
grows.

TOPANGA DAWN

The birds are singing,
awakening with the sun
once again, singing loudly, fully,
hundreds in unison, invisible
amongst eucalyptus leaves.

I do not know their names
but each morning, unfettered,
their song soars, precisely
as the first rouge of dawn
paints the hills, and suddenly
moments later, once light
is greeted, they stop.

What great wonder gives
this moment? What ignites
this daily chorus,
this bright celebration?

Caught listening in awe
their music inspires how we too
might rise each day simply,
without thought, and rejoice
at the mere gift of waking.

Their singing teaching a way
to answer the call of each
new day; to awaken joyfully,
wholehearted in song,
simply responding to light;

and with our breath,
connecting again
with the cyclic rhythm and return,
of this rising brightness
over which we have no say.

No say, except perhaps
to surrender,
and in surrendering,
to sing that one song
we are each here to sing—
full bodied, belted out, unleashed
into trees and wind and sun.

And in such singing come
to find ourselves at last
joining in with that one call,
the very one we came to make,
and the only One, which once begun,
makes a harmony of all Life:

a symphony of songs!

MORNING GLORIES

This morning
in triumph,
having completely
climbed the
chain-link fence,
they face the sun.

Translucent and open-mouthed,
their soft purple flesh
barely quivers in the breeze,
as they greet the morning;
these delicate petals
cheering in the glory
of Nature's win.

Having crawled
all the way up,
they now cover silver wire
in green and violet grace,
laughing
in the face
of man's metal
illusion
of control
and ownership.

DEAD FAWN

Cracked, her life cracked; belly torn
open, tiny ribs barely still,
exposed—and red, red flesh ripped.
I tripped as I came upon her,
my first encounter with such a warm
death, as if the predator crouched yet
behind some pine, dying for dusk
and return. Her head and legs are whole-
a 'clean kill'–flesh into flesh.
The head lies poised;
such a peaceful gaze stuns me.
No glaze of horror here, no flies no
vulture knows yet, but I.

My presence a mystery here,
feeling both one with yet somehow
outside this natural order. I see
but resist this death; I cannot
know it. I seem to have none, yet am
predator. I struggle valiantly within
to replace flesh and cover it, cover it
with skin, soft brown fur and spots,
to bring it again wobbling to its knees,
to stand it at last at the doe's heels,
to make it all
to make it all whole:
to make it alive again.

THE RIPENING

Reaching up blind,
up deep into laden
branches, fingers
barely brushing
soft round fuzz;

how easily
each plump,
fully-ripened
yellow-red peach
simply
drops;
coming free
at the slightest touch,
pulled down by
the mere weight
of its own readiness,
falling
into our open hands.

May we come
to learn
the peach tree's
natural
patience
and wisdom:

allowing for
the full ripening
of the deepest
questions,

so they may
grow juicy and full
in their own time,
whole, sweet and ready,
dropping easily,
naturally,
each
into their own
perfect
moment of harvest.

METAMORPHOSIS: WOMEN

Slipping slowly from the chrysalis,
tender and wet wings
begin to flit in the sun,
drying.

Being newborn
to such freedom,
this metamorphosis,
leaves us raw.

After years dreaming
in the dark cocoon,
(shifting tightly around
in shadowy movement),
suddenly, a terrifying wonder,
an inevitable opening out
into light,
finally freed
for unlimited possibilities
of flight.

Soon the strange
new beauty we are
will be whole
and this quiet time
of wings uncurling,
drying in the sun,
done.

We are called to flight,
to soaring.

Centuries crawling caterpillar style,
years in cocoon,
seem now no preparation
for such liberation.

So, we linger here
savoring the moment,
knowing that soon,
in that first flutter,
we will be off;

trusting Nature
to set the course
and our unfamiliar wings
to lift this new light body
aloft, as it is pulled,
inexorably, toward
the bright center
of the unknown.

Being drawn
to some sweet nectar
hidden amidst
spring's first blossoms,

we enter
our true work—
simply feeding
and thus
being fed—

drawn ultimately
into our brief part
in re-flowering
the whole garden.

"ETERNAL IDOL"
Sculpture
A. Rodin, 1889, (6 x 6 x 3)

If statues could speak
words would say no more
than your bronzed body—
a sphinx—
suspended here in time,
its word
filling space
with shape.

Yours is touch,
gazing with silent eyes filled,
your man pressed against you—
half-leaning, half-kneeling—
gently planting a kiss there,
where it may grow when you part,
tucked beneath your left breast,
upon your heart.

    Woman,
I know in you all women,
        recognize in this moment
        those eyes
        which contain all touch, falling
        beyond the head buried in you,
        beyond his arms, crossed behind
        restrained as in reverence
        from ardor.

        Artists have always praised you —
        those individual bodies posed for eternity
        in bronze and clay

etched and in oil; images cut
to withstand the soil
of time.

Woman, mankind will enter you
always
in wedding beds,
in churches, in brothels,
in worship of all kinds
(at times unkind)
for your eternal depths,
your dark body,
are the shape of Mystery
for all men.

*   *   *   *

Woman, I discover
my part in you
each day when I rise
and touch my man
through those same bronze
eyes.

BEYOND THE SEA OF FEAR

She stretches poised,
shimmering in lime green lycra,
far beyond the sea of fear.
No net, no guy-wires beneath,
poised perfectly,
this tiny acrobat balances
on one hand, upside down,
upon a tiny platform high
above the Circque du Soleil stage.
Each motion, a new grace,
bending at the waist,
her lithe body horizontal,
she moves in impossible flexion
circling sidewise and around,
slowly, making a new agreement
with gravity;
as she turns,
her slow-motion dance
flows,
completely controlled
yet fluid and free.

With strength and courage
her slow dance
beckons us all to step
beyond our tiny limited world,
outside our own sea of fear;
it calls us to stretch,
to step beyond
where we now swim, beyond
all we know as real and possible
to go beyond

what we call our world,
to poise ourselves,
to go, for once
as she does,
outside the known—
risking
the impossible—
living this way
wherever we can.
Now.
Being
at last
fully
alive.

ALL TOO SOON

All too soon
we will each wake up,
and looking in the mirror,
be strangely startled
by what we see.

This evening, the face
of the aged one on the street,
bent, hobbling slowly over his cane,
the one who, out of fear
we don't really see--
the one who often feels alone
and quite invisible--
appears as if in a dream.

In no time, such a face
will gaze back from the glass
at us. And though it all happened
gradually, still,
we will be surprised
by grey hair, lines
and sagging places,
because in our deepest hearts
we will not feel old.

That which was never born
and never dies will see freshly
this strange yet familiar face
looking back, puzzling
over how quickly
it all went;
how peculiar

seeing this reflection,
while still being
somehow that one
(untouched, unchanging)
who has always looked.

No matter how old
or how youthful,
our features now,
no matter that we may
long to look away
from our aging body
in this era infatuated
with youth,
nonetheless, all too soon,
a day will come when
we may each wake up
startled by what we see.

Today there is still time
to turn toward what we might
easily avoid, still a chance
to reach out and embrace,
to hold in our palms a dear aging face,
to plant a kiss gently on her cheek;
time to take a wrinkled hand in ours,
or simply offer a bright smile,
a warm "Good morning"
as we pass by.

With such plain gestures,
with such simple compassion,
we prepare for a moment,
when perhaps,
we can come to love it all:

the wisdom etched in each line,
knowing at the same time
that ageless radiant beauty
which no mirror can ever show.

FINAL MOVE

Dad came downstairs
moving slowly now,
with a letter in hand
long forgotten, just found.

A pause in the midst
of paper purging,
preparing to leave
the family home
we loved
after 48 years,
many gatherings,
3 children,
well nourished gardens,
1 cat
1 dog
many squirrels and bluejays.

Holding back tears,
his hand shook a bit,
presenting the yellow paper:
her first love letter to him
53 years ago.

Stopping
to honor
the bitter sweet joy
of the moment
and such rare endurance
of heart,
they touch,

and time
also stops:

bowing
to that
Love
which
outlasts
all.

NANA'S GRACE
(for my grandmother)

Tonight over tea,
sitting upon
the tall slatted chairs
in that ageless kitchen,
where yellow-orange fruits
dance still on white walls,
we touched
and speaking in dreams
felt the half-century
(once an ocean between)
shrink to only a cup.

I've seen no brown-tinged
photo from your youth, yet
I've known those ageless
eyes (a blue only babies have
but lose) unframed by lens;
seen that hair, blonde as
wild oats in June, months
before the first snow.

These bits of you and more
came back: your love of
language and fathomless
laugh coming always
from a sense of being
in touch with something
much larger than your-
self.

Tonight a full solstice moon
shines white in your hair;
and the instigation of a poem,
lived but never written,
somehow now becomes this
(in my blood) from you my
soft benefactress.

SPRING SCULPTURE: CALIFORNIA

Where we lie deep green in grass

      white oak bends to ground, barren.
      Convoluted from root to sky and now
      to earth again, old bones bow,
      greyed and yielding—
      seed's sculpture in its dying years.

            A mocking bird echoes
            overandoverandover
            piping from the dying oak
            mimicries to allure
            a mate; trilling the scores
            in twosthreesfours.

Grass fringes this trunk now prone
upon its deathbed. It might
live years yet while these roots,
crouched like crocodile haunches
draw still. Amongst scalloped leaves
death has begun to show, first
in frail branches as diseased globes,
brown and black.

            At last she responds and flies
            riding the rush of March wind,
            tracing the beckoning cries
            from tree to tree to him.

And meadow green rises
in ripples and falls
with mating songs. While
above, in the frail tracery,
they mold a nest of
twigsandgrassandleaves.

Here below, we lie deep;
casting a mold with our bodies
making a wedding bed of this grass—
now crushed and shining.

IN LUXEMBOURG GARDENS

That glance, grey as her stony non-movements
penetrates. Sometimes I feel as statuesque
as she. Maybe she moves (when I look away)
to glance at my self statue.

    Everything changes, moves, becoming
    the same. The fountain turns, and spraying
    falls where it fell before. The pigeon pecks
    then perches on her head, and head cocked,
    he glares, glutton in mockery of her immobility:
    his pedestal
    her head,
    hers, square quartz,
    mine—a green iron chair.

Immobile, I move through appearances,
sculpted and sculpting that which will wear
time's pecks better than I.

YEARNING

We are all learning,
learning to lean,

learning to lean
all the way in,
into the depths
of this yearning.

The wind sings
in its free and full
blowing over the ocean:

watch how the white sail
fills and bends, billowing
above the bow
as it keels way over,
cutting into the blue,
held there,
suspended by
an invisible fullness,
a taut surrender
into a moment-
by-moment edge.

Riding the mystery,
riding out the waves;
so we are learning
how to lean
into the waves
of seeming separation,
finding our edge,
letting go,

going with the wind
leaning into loss,
letting it fill us,
learning to ride
until at last
all gives way
into a deep Oneness.

From this place
there is nothing
that cannot be used
to blow us open wildly,
into the wideness,
into the vastness of Love,
into the wholeness
we already
always are.

SCULPTURE:

"SHE WHO ONCE WAS THE HELMET-MAKER'S BEAUTIFUL WIFE"

A. Rodin, Bronze, Before 1885 (20 x 10 x 12)

Bent, broken woman scare-crow
doubled in despair, decrepitude;
with what sunken sadness you
contemplate your withered state.

A wisp in the face of decay you gaze
wistfully over that corpse-cover,
down desiccated breasts, stretched
belly to grape-vine legs.

An aged courtesan, you came to town
seeking your lost son. Now in bronze
your skin sags into rock
at heel, hand and buttock.

Italian, like Donatello's Magdalene,
you fell to want and sought Rodin,
moving his hand, his mind to mold
"regrets de la Belle Heaulmiere..."

You never knew a helmet-maker,
never knew Donatello or Villon;
but loss you have known—it is written in
wrinkles: beauty, and a son.

Yet the ageless light that shines
unweathered through your timeless gaze
still conveys that which remains ever
untouched by years, months or days.

TOPANGA TWILIGHT

Walking uphill
inside the great intimacy
of it All, walking
into the timeless awe
of twilight between worlds
I drink in this moment,
gazing up toward horizon's
jagged edge: one
immense translucent sky
greets the long dark line
of trees across the canyon.

Here, inside that place
where silence deepens
and takes over,
(moving in and as that peace),
even two does with fawn
are unmoved as I approach
their open field.

Without words
they know it.
This great intimacy
with All
in which they live
is a harmony
binding them to life.
Such peace is their home,
and sensing this
they look up, only briefly,
as if seeing a bird
or rabbit pass by,
and continue to graze.

All is gratefulness:
to be
so blessed by Nature,
to be
simply here
amongst them,
one of them,
for a moment
free and quiet
just passing by
and yet somehow
at one with it All.

STARRY NIGHT

Tonight upon the deck,
glancing up,
stopped cold,
breathing in
the sparkling beauty
of stars, as if for the first time,
I am taken over by their
still motion, by their bright
electric dance,
by sheer illumination—
a pure vibrancy
peeking through
blue-black sky-waters.

And then the Heart,
like some ancient
crusty sea chest,
swings open wide,
as this ocean of stars
with all their flickering light,
collects at once,
like eternal
shimmering jewels
held inexplicably both
within and without.

The call of such
a moment cannot be
sought, coming as it does
inexplicably.

And a treasure chest
such as this—
filled with galaxies
both still and radiant—
asks only to be left
forever opened,
available for all.

ETERNAL NOW

What if we are alive, even now,
in the bliss of the Buddha's smile;
or in the shining light that sparkles
from an ancient sage's eye?

What if, in Truth, we are nothing less
than what moved Christ's hand to bless;
or if, even now, we abide in what gives
the silent grace of a guru's glance?

What if when we move, it flows
from the same pure heart that gives
a monk impetus to bow; or from
the strong silent center the Sufi's
ecstatic dance whirls around?

What if our speaking emanates
from the same profound source that
sounds the Shaman's sacred drum?

or if we are actually still, while in midst
of movement, suspended, like the iridescent
red breast of a hummingbird, hovering
motionless, amidst her wing's humming?

What if, all the while, we are always
both awake, and awakening,
the way each blossom opens to sun
amongst all that daily dawns, dancing on,
in infinite forms through time?

What if…?

IN THE WAKE

In the wake of awakening,
waves part,
peaking and churning,
as the bright ship
of grace sails on.
Behind her stern
white foam parts
building and cresting,
it rolls up and over,
dissolving,
washing around
and through,
then slowly,
gradually,
rolling ripples
begin to ease down.

As her pure white sail
slips silently out of sight
beyond the thin line
of horizon,
waves soften
to small rolling swells,
gently rising and falling,
finally falling flat,
sinking at last
into vast stillness.

Now
only the boundless living ocean.
Now, even in midst of storm,
only clear calm waters

and silent depths beneath,
now only one sea,
one essence present
everywhere;
in stillness,
in motion,
only one
eternal
peace.

THE PATH

If a man wishes to be sure of the road
he treads on, he must close his eyes and
walk in the dark.
        — St. John of the Cross

There is a path
in the dark fields
of silence.
Unlit, unmarked,
step by blind step
it appears only when
we are surely lost,
lost completely.

With eyes closed
(even in the dark),
letting soles of feet
be the guide,
tentative at first,
slowly we come
to trust them to feel
the way forward,
to move naturally,
gently, sensing
the ground beneath.

Surrendering step by step
knowing nothing,
gradually, each stride
shows the way;

each
it's own
simple unfolding,
with no thought,
nor anything
even
remotely
like
knowing.

LIKE SKY

Today, like sky,
I am free,
and let any thoughts be
as they drift
in wispy clouds,
by a pure blue screen.
Then, all at once,
completely serene,
the heavens clear.

Today, I am like ocean,
remembering that it forgot
and thought itself
to be only a wave.

Today my only address
is eternity,
and from this place
I know all that is,
as within this sea.

Today, being free
of all notions,
seeing
in all other waves
ocean too;
the illusion
"you" and "I"
washes away.

Today I am free,
awake,
and grateful
to simply Be.

(for Thich Nhat Hahn)

REVELATION

It seems as if it happens all at once.

Like last night when
thrashing winds
of a December storm,
blew away the bougainvillea
which completely covered
the kitchen skylight--
lifting it completely off.

Suddenly today
a shocking brightness
fills the entire room.

Unexpectedly, everything shines
plainly, simply as it is.

A welcome lightness of being
as sun illuminates iridescent
red poinsettia petals, pierces
into cabinet corners,
revealing hidden dust and grime
not apparent in the lesser light;
illuminating all equally.

It seems like it happens all at once.
Yet I know, in a place already loosened,
softened, by gentler breezes,
this was just the final blow.

Now a presence of peace pervades
and an awareness that

it could not be otherwise
(being held as it is
within a deeper peace),

and that through grace,
such realization comes to all,
and in its own time,

> at times in midst of
> a chaos of great winds
> and sometimes in the quiet fall
> of a first cautious step
> gently entering
> the silent unknown.

Simply weathering our storms,
enduring, letting them
deepen and open us,
it seems,
that even if unsought,
peace does come in the end.

This which we are, seeks us out,
this which transcends all storms,
awakens us in mercy and grace.

> In any moment,
> at any time, in any place,

> revelation
> awaits.

DEVOTION

It's all an offering now,
too intimate for speech,
yet somehow, somewhere
an invisible bow.
Even in the flow
of the everyday,
washing the floor,
arranging roses and daisies;
a growing devotion,
simply Being
awash in an ocean
of grace and bliss
beyond all knowing,
beyond all sense.

Imperceptible
in the midst of it all
something like
a small smile curls:
an unseen bow
to the Great Thou
to the Unseen One:
I Am, we all are, it all Is.

In stillness, a sudden wonder:
the radiance of droplets
watering jasmine,
and a soaring, riding the edge of a breeze,
a rustling of dusty branches arises

and at that place where
language fails,
instantly,
nothing is
ever the same…

At once, our dream world of time
is revealed.
Here, impossibly one with,
and yet beyond
this precious, this ordinary
moment:
                seer and seen
                One,
                silent, unmoved,
                I Am.

INCENSE BURNING

As each ash
drops away into
absolute
stillness,
all thoughts once
solid, certain, real,
dissolve: drift down
falling one by one
soundlessly
to sand.

Only a faint trace
of path remains in this
rising ripple of smoke,
lingering in the pure
scent of peace,
in deep silence,
a bliss
forged in this
emptiness
where once desire's
glowing embers burned
recklessly toward
some dreamy end.

Lightly,
sacred remnants
flutter down like
tiny grey feathers
from a soaring bird,
dropped in offering,
in celebration of life's
longing for Self,

now fallen, full
and free.

As the last notion fades
"I" fall through into
nothing;
leaving behind
only ashes
resting
invisible
in sand.

(For Ramana Maharshi)

MESSAGE FOR OUR TIMES

Despite the headlines
we need not fear the future,
for there will always be
those Ones
whose names and unseen
holy work for unity
don't make evening news.
And there will always be
this same holiness
nested within the heart
of each of us who lives.

When we courageously
surrender all fear and hope,
to a love of what is eternal,
and (not stopping even at bliss),
encounter just beyond this,
an ever-present sea
of peace and quietude—
that still sea upon which even
our most turbulent times
seem to float and shift.

From the base of such
depth and equanimity we
can move in the world,
engaging fully
not as savior or saint,
but transparently,
the way pure mists
drawn upward from seas
rain down,

penetrating again gently,
fully nourishing Earth.
Such equanimity
grounds and holds all motion
the way even oceans' immense depths
are bound beneath by solid sand and stone.

With deepening awareness
we each appear as
wholeness at play:
as if having forgotten
Self for a long day,
dreaming
some dream of separativity.

*   *   *   *

Now a horn sounds
awakening,
marking the beginning
of a new era, a new day.

Will we walk together
onto the green fields of greatness
taking hold the gauntlet of Unity
just as we are, participating
with whatever possibility we see?
Will we work together at last
weaving peace and sustainability
from the truth of our oneness
with courage and strength,
for our children, our earth, for all Life--
        all the while resting peacefully, lightly,
        in the lap of Eternity?

SISTER

Brakes screeching
the big blue bus swings wide
and she reaches over—
black arms stretching long
around the huge horizontal wheel—
she's glistening and beautiful even
behind the darkest shade of shades.

Rounding the corner
she is strong.

Sister, I see you.
I long for a healing song
our hearts can learn
and sing together.
But I don't have the words
and I can't find you.

Stop. I see them.
On those other corners
our children are hanging, waiting.
They want to know:
will we step out of time?
Will we do it?

They say they don't care
about the words—
just sing—
they told me
they cannot
wait
much
longer.

DARE WE IMAGINE

Dare we imagine

    the pink dawn of a day
    when what we do and say
    are in complete
    harmony with earth
    and each other,
    when all life as we know it
    is no longer in jeopardy?

Dare we see that dawn now,
even in blackest night,
dare we seek and live for those
faint glints of soft light, of a new morn?

Given our global crises,
there are always the easy ways out:
to freeze or play dumb,
to numb out, or deny
and go back to bed,
pulling the cozy blanket
of "business as usual"
over our head.

It's time to wake up, to open
our eyes, to extend our sight,
daring to see on the horizon,
(even now through thickest night),
our children's bright eyes shining.

Standing boldly
in this future light
we must dare to see

far beyond them
to their children, waiting,
thrusting small hands back
through illusory time,
hearts trusting,
reaching out,
asking us each
to rise and speak
(or even shout)
to both be and act for them,
to envision each day
the birth of a new possibility
as our future reality:

> *Our blue-green planet*
> *sustained by reverence for all life,*
> *a home where acting in accord*
> *with earth and generations hence,*
> *honoring our interdependence,*
> *we weave a human bond*
> *that reaches like a song far beyond*
> *time and surface difference—*
> *living, working, together,*
> *surmounting obstacles,*
> *being as One.*

Imagine who we will be,
who humanity will be,
on the dawn of that day…

A GREAT LOVE

In silence
there lives

a great Love.

This is our true
home.

There it all
began

and no matter
what happens
        (in the in-between)
there it all returns
in the end.

Author's Biography

Jane Palmer began writing poetry as a teenager. Her writing was always given by a love of language and the challenge of expressing the inexpressible. While attending Edinburgh University for a year of study abroad, she began writing seriously and published her first poem.

Returning from Scotland and encouraged by Scots poet Norman McCaig, she was accepted into Stanford University's Master's Program in Creative Writing where she studied with English poet Donald Davie and published her second poem. After graduating, Jane remained at Stanford to teach Creative Writing at the university as a Jones Fellow, as well as through community programs with women in East Palo Alto.

After a profound experience of awakening in the early 1970s, Jane decided to see if she could contribute more fully that which was being expressed only in poetry. She stopped writing in 1972 and entered a new life of public service, facilitating transformational programs around the world for thousands of people.

More than twenty years later at the completion of that active work with individuals and organizations, her poetry began to flow again, now enriched by years of working profoundly and intimately with so many people. While living alone and close to nature, Jane began a whole new period of solitude and deep meditation. This time included being profoundly touched and moved by the wonder of nature, the great mystic poets and writers, and her own spiritual teachers.

Singing from Silence is a portion of the over 140 poems that emerged during that time. They are an invitation for us all to take time in our current harried era for solitude and silence; an offering of a peace available to all in the simple practice of taking time to stop, be still, and listen deeply.

www.ingramcontent.com/pod-product-compliance
Lightning Source LLC
Chambersburg PA
CBHW071147090426
42736CB00012B/2264